Text copyright © 2021 by Willie Nelson and Bobbie Nelson
Jacket art and interior illustrations copyright © 2021 by Kyung Eun Han

All rights reserved. Published in the United States by Doubleday, an imprint of Random House Children's Books,
a division of Penguin Random House LLC, New York. Brief portions of this work appeared in significantly different form in
Me and Sister Bobbie: True Tales of the Family Band by Willie Nelson and Bobbie Lee Nelson with David Ritz, copyright © 2020 by
Willie Nelson and Bobbie Lee Nelson. Published in the United States in hardcover by Random House,
an imprint and division of Penguin Random House LLC, New York, in 2020.

Doubleday and the colophon are registered trademarks of Penguin Random House LLC.

Visit us on the Web! rhcbooks.com

Educators and librarians, for a variety of teaching tools, visit us at RHTeachersLibrarians.com

Library of Congress Cataloging-in-Publication Data is available upon request.
ISBN 978-1-9848-5183-3 (trade) — ISBN 978-1-9848-5184-0 (lib. bdg.) —
ISBN 978-1-9848-5185-7 (ebook)

MANUFACTURED IN CHINA
10 9 8 7 6 5 4 3 2 1
First Edition

Willie Nelson & Bobbie Nelson

Sister, Brother, Family

An American Childhood in Music

Co-written by Chris Barton

Illustrated by Kyung Eun Han

Doubleday Books for Young Readers

WILLIE

Long before our bus began to roar down this highway—before there even *was* a highway—we were just a sister and brother.

A girl who fell in love with the sound of a piano. A boy who fell for the guitar.

We loved music. Music loved us back.

It provided for us and protected us and supported our family's soul.

It still does.

Soon, people will arrive for our show.

Soon, Bobbie and I will start making music.

Just like we always have.

BOBBIE

My first piano was one we made from cardboard, with a keyboard drawn in crayon.

Willie and I would sit under our peach tree for hours, singing while I played.

That piano didn't make a sound, except in our minds.

I couldn't wait for the real thing.

Willie and I had always lived in little Abbott, Texas. We ate food our family grew and attended church every Sunday and Wednesday.

We were raised by our grandparents Mama and Daddy Nelson. Daddy Nelson was a blacksmith, and Mama Nelson tended the home when she wasn't out picking cotton or corn.

We had so little money but so much love.

WILLIE

And so much music.

Music from the church. Music from our neighbors. And most of all, music from Mama and Daddy Nelson.

I saw him as the strongest man in the country, and her as the sweetest woman on God's green earth.

The garden behind our little house yielded tomatoes, turnips, lettuce, and green peas. We had a couple of hogs and a few calves. Always enough to eat.

Our grandparents were always singing. They'd study music by lantern light, then turn around and teach Sister and me. That's one way they showed their love for us.

Every so often, we'd go to an all-day singing and dinner on the ground. A big picnic, basically, with hymns and fellowship.

The feeling of all those people joining in on "Will the Circle Be Unbroken?" got into my soul and never left.

BOBBIE

When Daddy Nelson took me to a gospel-singing convention, it was the piano playing that grabbed me. And at our church, I watched in wonder as Miss Bertha May's fingers flew over all those keys. Then she and Mama Nelson asked if I could imitate that.

I could. The piano felt like a friend.

BOBBIE

Daddy Nelson went to the general store, paid five dollars toward an old upright piano, and brought it home. He told me, "Play till your heart's content." And I did. Mama Nelson taught me how.

At first, I worried that Brother might be jealous, but there was nothing to worry about. Willie was born secure.

WILLIE

Eighty-eight keys were fine for Bobbie but way too many for me. Six strings seemed just about right, so our grandparents bought me a guitar from the Sears catalog.

Daddy Nelson showed me how to make it sing. That guitar became a part of me.

I'd been writing poems, and I had a funny feeling that the words were supposed to go with music. Now I could make that happen.

My life was pretty rosy, at least until age six.

BOBBIE

Then came a terrible blow.

Daddy Nelson got sick. And then, quickly, he was gone.

During his last hours, Daddy Nelson called me to his bedside.

"Play me a song, Bobbie," he said. "Play 'I'll Fly Away.'"

I went to the piano, and as I played, Mama Nelson and Willie sang along.

"Some glad morning when this life is over, I'll fly away. . . ."

WILLIE

Daddy Nelson's death hit me hard. He had been stolen from us. We had been cheated.

But Sister made it clear we'd get through this together.

Where did she get that confidence and strength?

BOBBIE

I couldn't imagine the world without Daddy Nelson. But making music together was a source of comfort. It reassured us.

As much as I could, I kept Willie close to me, just as Mama Nelson kept us close to her.

The three of us would play "The Great Speckled Bird" just like that: close together, as a family. As Mama Nelson sang, she told Willie and me which chords came next.

Every now and then, his eyes met mine, and we lit up inside. Music made us feel connected to something bigger out there.

WILLIE

Still, with Daddy Nelson gone, there were holes to fill.

Our Philco radio helped, pulling in sounds from Chicago to Mexico.

To finish paying for Bobbie's piano, Mama Nelson sold a calf. To make ends

meet, she taught music to other kids, worked in the fields, and traded eggs from our

chickens for goods from the general store.

BOBBIE

When we came home in the evening, Mama Nelson made dinner and sang hymns. Her voice filled the house with love.

Then she read the Bible in her rocking chair. There, she taught me to braid her hair, and I taught Willie.

We took turns braiding. Like music, it was a ritual that brought calm and peace and held our family together.

BOBBIE

Making music wasn't something we did only at home. It seems we were always performing.
We played at first for Sunday services at church, then for dances at school.

It was an easy jump from "What a Friend We Have in Jesus" to "Waltz Across Texas," so if
kids wanted to boogie-woogie or jitterbug, Brother and I could get 'em going.

WILLIE

Not long after Daddy Nelson died, a fifteen-member family polka band kindly invited me to join them.

In front of a swirling dance-hall crowd, I was surrounded by fiddles, oompah horns, and big, loud drums. I had a blast.

What's more, it was the first time I ever got paid for making music.

WILLIE

Mama Nelson wasn't happy about me playing music for a dance hall full of adults.

Then I handed her eight dollars.

She was surprised. Eight dollars was my pay for working the fields for a week.

She wanted to know how long I had to work to earn that much.

"One night," I said.

She didn't say another word.

BOBBIE

Before long, Mama Nelson had to make peace with both her grandchildren playing in dance halls.

I guess she knew that no matter where we performed, Brother and I would be carrying a good message and making people happy.

BOBBIE

Family and music have been one and the same ever since Mama
Nelson placed my hands on the keys of a piano, and Daddy Nelson
put a guitar in Brother's arms.

Music has been our way of feeling, giving, and receiving love.
It sustains us to this day.

WILLIE

More than eighty years after Sister and I started playing music, we're still at it. There's no stronger, longer, or steadier relationship in my life.

When I go out there every night and look over, there she is.

And when we end our shows with "Will the Circle Be Unbroken?" and "I'll Fly Away," Mama and Daddy Nelson are right there, too.

As long as there's music, our family will always be together.